MW01490617

The Scanner Monkey Way

Sharing with a Tribe of Online Sellers to
Make More Money and Have More Fun

Jay Bayne
Cordelia Blake

SMLLC Press, Houston, TX

2014

LAURA, THANKS FOR BEING A VALUED MEMBER OF THE SCANNER MONKEY TRIBE! MONKEY ON!

Jay Bayne

The Scanner Monkey Way:

Sharing with a Tribe of Online Sellers to Make More Money and Have More Fun

Bayne, Jay

Blake, Cordelia

Copyright © 2014 Jay Bayne. All rights reserved.

Edited by Rebecca Smotherman

Published by SMLLC Press, Houston, TX 77429

First Printing, August 2014

ISBN-13: 978-1500697310

ISBN-10: 1500697311

Printed in the United States of America

Cover photo by James Cowen

encourage electronic piracy of copyrighted materials. Your support of the author's rights is appreciated.

The publisher does not have any control over and does not assume any responsibility for third-party websites or their contents.

Amazon, Amazon.com, and Fulfillment By Amazon (FBA) are registered trademarks of Amazon.com, Inc. This book is not affiliated with nor endorsed by Amazon.

eBay and eBay.com are registered trademarks of eBay, Inc.

Scanfob is a registered trademark of Serialio.com. Bluetooth is a registered trademark of Bluetooth SIG, Inc.

All other names and trademarks are property of their respective owners.

Earnings Disclaimer

There is no promise or representation that you will make a certain amount of money, or any money, or not lose money, as a result of using the resources of Scanner Monkey.

As with any business, your results will vary and will be based on your personal abilities, experience, knowledge, capabilities, level of desire, and an infinite number of variables beyond our control, including variables we or you have not anticipated. There are no guarantees concerning the level of success you may experience. Each person's results will vary.

There are unknown risks in any business, particularly with online selling where advances and changes can happen quickly.

Dedications

From Jay Bayne,

My Family
This book is dedicated to my wife Karen and children Lauren, Cara, and Alex for putting up with me while I "do my monkey thing." None of this would be possible without your unwavering support. I love you all more than words can say!

I would also like to dedicate this book to the memory of my dad, Charles Bayne, who always told me that to be successful I need to surround myself with people that are smarter than me. Mission accomplished, Dad!

The "Crew"
Chris Green ("Godfather of Retail Arbitrage") – I am forever in your debt. Thank you for your advice, motivation, guidance, and most importantly, your friendship.

Duane Malek ("Mr. Fast Turn") and Karin Isgur Bergsagel ("Mother Hen") – I cannot thank you both enough for all of your helpful feedback and support over the last year.

The Scanner Monkeys
Thanks to all of the Scanner Monkey members who took a leap of faith and embraced "the Scanner Monkey Way." Every day in every way you make me proud to be part of such a special community!

Last, but certainly not least, I would like to thank my co-author and co-leader Cordelia Blake for coming into my life at just the right time and helping me to materialize my vision.

From Cordelia Blake,

My Family

Everything I do is dedicated to my wonderful family, my two boys Alexander and Maxwell and my husband Mike.

Everything I do is always dedicated to my wonderful father, Robert Zaslavsky. He dedicated his first book (and really his whole life) to me, so I will dedicate mine to him. He has always been there for me and showed me that through all of life's difficulties being smart and funny helps tremendously!

"You have begot me, bred me, loved me: I
Return those duties back as are right fit,
Obey you, love you, and most honour you."
-*King Lear*, William Shakespeare

Hey Hey - To The Monkeys

Without getting too schmaltzy here, Jay - you're a mensch. Monkeys - being part of a group that is all about helping each other has literally changed my life. I thank you all.

Foreword – Chris Green

I've known Jay for a while now, and we've become good friends outside the world of Amazon and FBA. Having watched the formation and evolution (see what I did there?) of his Scanner Monkey group, or tribe, I am very certain of one thing: Jay genuinely cares about the well-being of each and every member of his tribe. He wants to provide them with true value to help their businesses. Jay has a passion for helping others, and that spirit is evident in everything that he does.

I remember the day that Jay called me with his original idea for Scanner Monkey very well. You see, I'm known as the Godfather of FBA, author of *Arbitrage*, and co-founder of ScanPower, but a trademark lawyer? Not so much. That's why I thought it was a little bit funny when Jay asked me if I knew if anyone had trademarked the term Scanner Monkey. I had no idea, but my first suggestion to him was to check if the .com domain name was registered, and if it wasn't, that it was very likely not being used by anyone. Jay followed that up with the Facebook Page, Group, and Twitter, and through a little research, registered Scanner Monkey as his own trademark. Now Jay has written his own book, not just about what Scanner Monkey is, but the story and history of how Scanner Monkey came to be.

One reason that I am thrilled that Jay has written a book is to share the current value and future vision for this Scanner Monkey tribe. Jay currently shares so much information and provides so much value that it can be hard to keep track of everything. I also think that it is important to look back and remember how things got started, where things used to be, how people tried new things, and watch the evolution of the Scanner Monkey tribe.

Jay takes all the energy around him, (whether it is positive or negative) and turns it into motivation. His idea and subsequent creation of Scanner Monkey has helped hundreds, if not thousands, of Amazon sellers as well as pave the way for others to build online communities of online sellers. Jay is truly a pioneer, and I am thankful for his friendship.

Chris Green

Table of Contents

The Scanner Monkey Way

Chapter 1 – Hey, Hey We're the Monkeys!

Intro to Jay - by Cordelia

The Scanner Monkey group and philosophy was founded by part time online seller, Jay Bayne. I have only known him for a short time, but have been profoundly (and positively) influenced by him. He started Scanner Monkey because of his personal commitment to make the world, or at least his corner of it, a better place. He saw an opportunity to develop a community of professionals that would support, educate, entertain, and empower each other. Each person's success is seen as a contribution to everyone's success, rather than a threat to someone else's. He took a conversation and turned it into a life changing community that reaches across religions, personality types, genders, and nations.

I personally was struggling when I found Scanner Monkey. The group had just started around the same time that I was getting into the business of FBA (Fulfillment by Amazon). I was struggling to find items to source, and I felt isolated and alone working by myself at home all the time. I vividly remember trying to understand what type of items people were selling profitably and being told by veteran sellers to do my own work and figure it out.

When Scanner Monkey started I was thrilled to be a part of a group of people who would seriously answer that question about sourcing and so many more. As the group grew quickly, I reached out to Jay to help with some aspects of the group administration, and we struck up a friendship. I was then, and continue to be, inspired by his never ending positivity, honesty, professionalism, and kindness. I was given the chance to work for Scanner Monkey as the group grew and took the job to work with Jay. I would pretty much work for him doing anything. I consider him a friend, a mentor, and a tremendous leader. He pours his heart and soul into Scanner Monkey. He genuinely wants every member to receive value, and his passion, dedication, kindness, and humor are profoundly inspirational.

I am now a successful Amazon seller with a growing business and it is all due to the community of Scanner Monkey. I have made some true friends and am honored to be a part of the group in any role.

As the leader of our wonderful group, Jay holds himself to the highest standards ethically and professionally. I am deeply grateful for the part that Scanner Monkey and Jay have played in my family's and my life.

Cordelia Blake

Intro to Cordelia – by Jay Bayne

I first met Cordelia Blake in November 2013 in the Scanner Monkey Facebook group when she sent me a message with an offer to help with the group. She really didn't know me other than what I've posted within the group, but she sent several messages praising my efforts and offering suggestions on ways to make it better (tip: if you want to get to know me, starting with praise works every time). I could tell that Cordelia was a Scanner Monkey "ambassador" from the very beginning and was someone who shared my passion for developing a community of positive minded and supportive online sellers.

The Scanner Monkey Way

After a few dozen messages I asked Cordelia to call me on the phone. We both had so many ideas flying back and forth that it would have taken a couple of days via text messages to have the equivalent of a half hour phone conversation. I'll never forget my first phone conversation with Cordelia Blake. I was at Target sourcing the clearance sections with the "help" of one of my daughters (her version of help is repeatedly saying "I want that!" to everything I load in the cart). This was a significant conversation because it is when we first discussed creating a blog of all of the BOLOs shared in the Scanner Monkey Facebook group (discussed further in Chapter 10).

After talking to Cordelia for a few minutes I was immediately impressed with her knowledge of website development and technical expertise. I must admit this was an area where I was lacking in skills and was grateful to finally find someone that could walk me through the process of developing a web-based resource to back up the Facebook group.

The beginning of our relationship was limited to me saying "what about **this** idea?" and Cordelia walking me through how it could be done and what resources would be required to put it in place. After a while she was coming back to me with "what about **that** idea?" and I would figure out if it was within my budget.

It didn't take long for me to realize what a valuable asset Cordelia could be for Scanner Monkey. As a former trainer, website developer, business owner, and part-time online seller, she possessed the perfect skill set to help me take Scanner Monkey to the next level. It doesn't hurt that she is a genuinely nice person that the members of our group have come to admire and respect. In fact, she made such an impression on me that I made her an admin of the Scanner Monkey Facebook group within a couple of weeks after our first correspondence.

I can honestly say that the Scanner Monkey group wouldn't be where it is today if it wasn't for the input and influence of Cordelia! She has become the "yin" to my "yang," and it is very rare that I do anything related to the group without bouncing ideas off her first. I really can't imagine doing this without her...and I'm certain that the group feels the same way about their "Queen Monkey."

Jay Bayne

Chapter 2 - How to Use this Book

"Whenever you read a good book, it's like the author is right there, in the room talking to you, which is why I don't like to read good books."

Jack Handy
Deep Thoughts by Jack Handy

"The Scanner Monkey Way" is both a personal narrative describing the formation and philosophy of the Scanner Monkey group and an outline of the resources available to its members. The underlying theme throughout this book is how sharing information and working with others will help you increase your online sales on Amazon or eBay and grow your business.

"The Scanner Monkey Way" is **not** a how to guide with specific tips on reselling online through Amazon or eBay, but rather a summary of Scanner Monkey **resources** available to assist you in growing **your business**.

If you want an A to Z guide on buying and selling online, there are several written and online publications available. We've even recommended a few of our favorites in the "Resources" section at the end of the book.

This book was written for two groups of online sellers:

1) Those that are **unfamiliar** with the Scanner Monkey group and want to understand how living the "Scanner Monkey Way" can help them make more money and be happier.

2) Those that are **current** members of Scanner Monkey and want to learn more about the history of the group and would like a detailed guide of the resources available as part of their membership.

Depending on which camp you fall in, you may want to read the chapters in a different order (or even skip entire chapters altogether if you are already familiar with the information covered).

Here is the sequence of chapters that we recommend based on your situation:

If you are new to selling online and NOT a Scanner Monkey member:

Start with "Scanner Monkey Lingo" (Chapter 13) for a glossary of commonly used terms and acronyms in the world of online selling that you may not be familiar with. Then start from the beginning of the book and read forward.

Promo Code!

Can't wait to join the Scanner Monkey fun? Sign up here and receive a coupon code for 15% off your 1st year membership or lifeteime membership. Plus, free updates. Plus, bananas. (Ok, no actual bananas but lots of virtual ones).

http://scannermonkey.com/bookdiscount

If you are an experienced seller and NOT a member of Scanner Monkey:

Read the book from beginning to end. You may want to skip the "Scanner Monkey Lingo" chapter as you are most likely familiar with a majority of the terms defined...although, you might find the definitions of some of the more obscure terms to be interesting.

If you are currently a Scanner Monkey member:

Selecting which chapters you choose to read will depend on what interests you about Scanner Monkey. There are lots of personal stories chronicling the origin, history, and evolution of Scanner Monkey in the "Scanner Monkey Background" section. If the behind-the-scenes look at why and how it all started interests you, then this would be a great place to start. However, if you are already familiar with the backstory, then feel free to skip ahead to the "Scanner Monkey Resources" section to see a detailed analysis of the resources included in your membership. Lastly, since you are already familiar with the group, you may choose to skip the "Testimonials" chapter of the book (although it's possible that you may see your own name in print as the writer of one of those testimonials).

Chapter 3 – What the Heck is a Scanner Monkey?

"Scanner Monkey WAS a derogatory term used in the past by extremist/elitist type sellers who thought the marketplace was being flooded with all kinds of clueless people (newbies) with a phone and a scanner...now, [the Scanner Monkey group] has more successful members and a more positive, encouraging environment than most other groups."

Al Craig
Scanner Monkey Member

Before learning the Scanner Monkey way and reviewing the Scanner Monkey philosophy, I'm sure there are a few readers of this book that would like to know exactly *what the heck is a Scanner Monkey?* This is definitely a loaded question with several possible answers.

First and foremost, Scanner Monkey is a community of online sellers. We focus on being positive, helping each other, and everyone becoming more profitable. The name Scanner Monkey can also refer to one of our wonderful members. Our members are:

- Beginners or "newbies"
- Those with over $1 million per year in sales
- Part timers & full timers
- Women & men
- In their teens & into their 80s
- Multi-racial

Located all over the USA and some abroad

 So much more...

The history of the term Scanner Monkey is turbulent since previously, many members of online seller groups have viewed each other solely as competition and behaved accordingly. Scanner Monkeys are renegades, as will be demonstrated when we take a look down the Scanner Monkey timeline.

In The Beginning

Historically speaking, a Scanner Monkey was a derogatory term used by the "old school" book sellers to describe any newbie at a book sale using a scanner or PDA device to access current pricing on Amazon or other online selling platforms. They would then use this pricing to determine whether or not to purchase the book for reselling. If you listened carefully you could sometimes hear a close-minded seller saying "those [bleep], [bleep] scanner monkeys with their newfangled scanning devices are horning in on my book sales!"

Those days are over and now most online sellers, including the long-time experts, are embracing technology and utilizing scanners with smart phones to research products for resell on Amazon. This pricing and profitability research is done in mere seconds while scanning products at retail stores or thrift stores!

Now that it's acceptable and commonplace to use the latest technology to access pricing and profitability data to remain competitive, why should Scanner Monkey be a bad term? The quick answer: **it shouldn't**!

Jay's Story

After a profound personal experience, I realized that there was a growing community of "new school" sellers who just did things differently. They were team- and sharing- oriented and were believers in the "abundance principle." I will tell the details of this pivotal experience in the next section on the origin of our group. Suffice it to say, I came head to head with the "old school" and saw how I wanted to be a part of something different.

I love monkeys and having fun, so I decided to use this previously negative term and redefine it as a badge of honor. After all, I know lots of Scanner Monkeys that are admirable people who just want to make a full time or part time living selling products online. And most of them are having a blast doing it!

So how did I go about changing the perception of the term Scanner Monkey? The first thing I needed to do was determine if anyone owned the rights to the term "Scanner Monkey." At the end of September 2013 I had a conversation with Chris Green to ask if he knew if anyone owned the rights to the term Scanner Monkey. Most of you will know Chris as the author of *"Arbitrage: The authoritative guide on how it works, why it works, and how it can work for you"* and the founder of the ScanPower suite of sourcing, listing, and repricing tools (scanpower.com). Chris said he was not aware of anyone owning the term, much less using it in a positive way.

After doing some research I realized that the term was wide open, and I started on my mission to begin the "Scanner Monkey Revolution." On October 16, 2013, I purchased the domain name ScannerMonkey.com and started the Scanner

Monkey Facebook group (Chris Green was the second member...after me). Now that doesn't necessarily make me the **first** Scanner Monkey, but it might make me the first one to say it with **pride**!

Jay Bayne
The First Scanner Monkey Profile Picture

After I staked my claim on the internet (and the federal trademark office) with the Scanner Monkey website and Facebook group, I came up with a new multipronged definition that would be both meaningful and fun.

The NEW definition of Scanner Monkey:

Scanner Monkey [ˈska-nər muhng-kee] - noun

1) Someone who **goes bananas** for buying products at retail stores or online and reselling on Amazon or other online selling platforms.

2) A person who **embraces technology** - using scanners, smart phones, computers, and tablets to locate profitable products to sell online.

3) An online seller who is **constantly learning** and growing his or her business with other members of the Scanner Monkey tribe.

4) An online seller who **supports others** in the Scanner Monkey community (and beyond) while having fun and making money!

The Scanner Monkey Way

How to Spot a Scanner Monkey

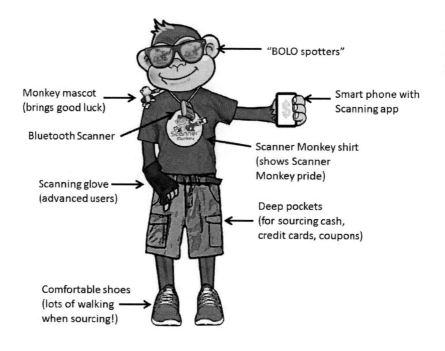

"BOLO spotters"

Monkey mascot
(brings good luck)

Smart phone with
Scanning app

Bluetooth Scanner

Scanner Monkey shirt
(shows Scanner
Monkey pride)

Scanning glove
(advanced users)

Deep pockets
(for sourcing cash,
credit cards, coupons)

Comfortable shoes
(lots of walking
when sourcing!)

Scanner Monkey
(scannius monkeyus ingeniusi)

Now that you know **what** a Scanner Monkey is, would you like to know **why** Scanner Monkey was founded in the first place? It all started when I was bitten by a radioactive monkey. Actually, that's not true...but wouldn't it be cool if it was? The origin story involves a little hardship, like the beginning of any Disney movie. But it also has a happy ending (and there was a little singing along the way).

The Scanner Monkey Way

Chapter 4 – The Origin of the Scanner Monkey Group

"This should be required reading for all new members of ScannerMonkey - our origin story, if you will. In the beginning, Jay Bayne created the #GreatBOLOWar."

James Baugh
Scanner Monkey Member

Once upon a time, Q4 of 2012 to be exact, there lived an Amazon third party seller named Jay Bayne, who sold mostly toys using Fulfillment by Amazon (FBA). Jay wanted to speed up the learning curve and quickly ramp up his business so he listened to all the pertinent podcasts, read FBA related books, and most importantly, participated in several online selling Facebook groups. These groups included *ScanPower, Thrifting for Profit*, and a few others. We find our hero, as we find many heroes, beginning a revolution with a simple question...

"Why?"

One fateful day I asked a question in the ScanPower Facebook group about a particular Doc McStuffins doll set that was listed on Amazon. The date was November 27, 2012 - right in the middle of the Q4 rush. The doll set in question had a product page on Amazon (ASIN: B008RBH156) with over 150 third party sellers at time of posting. However, Amazon itself did not carry this very popular set with an amazing ranking of under 1,000 in the toy category. **I inquired as to why** this was so and was quickly flamed in my post for "outing" this product that was already on most of the hot toy lists and several television commercials. In fact, this particular toy was discussed on the *Live with Kelly & Michael* show that same week!

My post received over 300 comments and was jokingly referred to as the start of the "Great BOLO Wars"! For those of you who are not familiar with the term **BOLO**, it stands for **Be On Look Out** for a product that could be resold online for a profit [BOLO trivia: it is also used by law enforcement agencies to "be on the lookout" for criminals].

I had opened up a virtual can of worms by posting a direct link to a product that several members of the group were already selling. I was accused by many of causing prices on this product to tank, and the posters certainly did not hide their disdain towards me. Here are just a few samples of the negative comments from the post (the names of the posters are withdrawn to protect the guilty):

- "Just keep your deals to yourself, don't try to be popular by talking about them and getting a couple people 'liking' your post. Selling on Amazon is a living for us...not a popularity contest."
- "My business won't be killed over this but it probably will be damaged even if only slightly."
- "You really are the stupidest seller on the planet, aren't you? Just because YOU sell out of a widget, no harm outing it to a group of 1000's of sellers, right? No harm screwing over the OTHER SELLERS ALREADY SELLING IT. No harm when the price tanks because 1000s of idiots who didn't know about it are now scrambling to find it?"

- 🍌 "Who cares if you just screwed over dozens of existing sellers on the widget when the price now tanks when the market floods? God save us all from the stupid sellers among us."
- 🍌 "The OP might be a genuinely nice person and simultaneously learning impaired."
- 🍌 "Stupid, stupid, stupid idea to post. I have no idea what the hell the op was thinking. People here are not your water-cooler associates - they are your competition!"

I still get a little emotional when I read these posts. After all, nobody likes to be called stupid! Obviously, I was pretty upset after receiving this online tongue lashing, and I asked Chris Green, the moderator of the group, to allow me to remove the post. He asked me to keep the post up, and rightfully so, because it was important to open up discussions like this so sellers can better understand both sides of the BOLO debate. I acquiesced, but it was tough because there were even more negative remarks directed towards me in the days to come.

More importantly, on the flip side, there were also members of the ScanPower group that showed compassion, support, and rationality. Here is a sampling of their comments that made it a little easier for me to keep up the post:

- 🍌 "This toy was on more hot lists than I can count and on TV programs...so it isn't like 'omg secret.' Same with Skylanders, and Furbies, and omg Monster High."
- 🍌 "This is nothing new. Booksellers who had spent years learning their trade felt the same way when 'scanner monkeys' came along with PDAs that told them everything from a book's barcode. There is nothing that could be done to prevent the new technologies from

taking hold. The traditional booksellers who survived and prospered adapted." [Interesting side note: this was the first time I saw the term Scanner Monkey used in a sentence]

🍌 "I don't think that Jay was trying to be 'cool' by posting this product, he was just asking a question. Don't start lashing out at someone and starting a fight over a question. He didn't tell everyone to go buy this, he was just wondering why Amazon wasn't taking advantage of a highly priced very popular toy."

🍌 "Sellers need to be aware that things like this will be shared, not just on Facebook. There are Facebook Groups of online sellers much bigger than this one, and also consider sites like FatWallet.com and SlickDeals.com. Someone could post that they found this item at Toys R Us for $29 and it's selling for $80 on Amazon and everyone who reads FatWallet (a lot) and everyone who has their Topic Alerts setup for keyword 'toys' (a lot) now knows about it (and that's a lot more than the members in this group)."

🍌 "I find sharing information is good karma, paying it forward, etc."

🍌 "If people are afraid of competition then they are in the wrong business."

🍌 "Competition is coming so adapt, adjust, innovate and compete. These are the only things that you control."

As you can see, sharing BOLOs was a very divisive topic, and both opponents and advocates of BOLOs dwelled together in the same groups on Facebook. During this time if someone was to share a BOLO in one of the groups, many times they would be reprimanded, flamed, or humiliated for outing a product that another seller may be selling. **This was the landscape at the time, and I wanted to change that!**

Surely, I wasn't the only one that felt this way. I had observed other positive thinking sellers in some of the groups. In fact, I had even come across a few other fun-loving jokesters in a couple of the Facebook groups.

I swore to myself that I would create a positive environment where positive minded sellers like these could gather and share their finds and advice without fear of negative feedback from other members. Additionally, I wanted to create a **fun** place where online sellers could gather and share interesting stories or successes from their day. Sometimes being an online seller can be a bit isolating if you are running the business by yourself. Online sellers should be able to experience the same camaraderie that one might find when working in an office with their co-workers. Perhaps I could create a group that encompasses that same feeling of fellowship.

I wanted to create a "virtual water cooler" where like-minded FBA sellers could gather and talk about their day. And so I created the Scanner Monkey Facebook group to help the **"Scanner Monkeys of the world unite!"** (tagline featured on our first banner seen below).

The Scanner Monkey Way

Since a few members of the ScanPower group really had my back in that post, I knew there would be support for creating a NEW group where members would feel comfortable sharing tips about sourcing, selling, and BOLOs with other members.

Over the course of the following year I compiled a list of names of positive minded and sharing members from different FBA and online selling related Facebook groups. These members would be the first ones I reached out to and would form the foundation of the new Scanner Monkey Facebook group (I fondly refer to them as the "founder monkeys").

With a lot of help from Chris Green about the basics of starting a Facebook group, I created the Scanner Monkey closed group in October of 2013. Chris was my first member, and I sent private messages to all of the potential "founder monkeys" asking if they would like to be a part of this positive, sharing, and caring community. Simultaneously, Chris announced the grand opening of Scanner Monkey in his ScanPower group. We had over 200 members join within a couple of days!

Within two weeks we had 600 members join the Scanner Monkey Facebook group and 20 to 30 BOLOs were posted by members every day (keep in mind this was also Q4, so there were plenty of BOLOs to post!). This was beyond my wildest expectations! Obviously, this was a concept whose time had come. Members were thrilled to finally have a place where they could freely post BOLOs without negative comments from other members (and if someone posted multiple negative comments, then they were immediately removed from the group).

It was then that I realized the true value of this crowd sourcing, so I decided to switch it to a paid membership group on November 1. This was one of the toughest decisions that I had to make concerning Scanner Monkey, but it was necessary for several reasons. First, members that pay for a service will value that service more than a member that does not pay. This also means they are more apt to participate in discussions within the group. Secondly, this would keep out the lurkers that were there simply to gain information with no intent to reciprocate with information of their own to share and that reciprocity is the very foundation of Scanner Monkey. Lastly, I was spending so much time working on the group and developing other value added services that I had very little time to source for my own FBA business. It was only fair that I should be compensated for my time moderating the group and for planning, marketing and coordinating other resources for the Scanner Monkeys.

I thought the paid membership would be an issue with the members, but to my surprise they agreed that the information being shared was certainly worth the price of admission. Many of the members have even said that they made up their membership fees several times over by finding a single profitable BOLO shared in the group.

After several discussions with a couple of my Scanner Monkey confidants, I set the original membership price at a measly $36.50 for the entire year (a mere dime a day). The membership fee has since risen to $99/year as additional services and features were added...and it remains at that same price to this day.

So there you have it, dear monkeys - the origin story of Scanner Monkey. What started as a negative response to a reasonable question, ended up as a much needed community which thrives on sharing, caring, and having fun in the process! Simply put, it was just the right time for the creation of Scanner Monkey.

And, in the words of French writer Victor Hugo, "There's nothing more powerful than an idea whose time has come."

I would like to add that I don't hold any ill will towards the people that lashed out against me in the post. I believe that everything happens for a reason and although the comments in the post were negative, it resulted in several more positive members banding together to form a unique alliance and community.

Postscript

This infamous post is still alive and kicking to this day because every once in a while a Scanner Monkey will bump it up for nostalgia sake. As far as the Doc McStuffins fiasco is concerned, the selling price on the doll remained pretty consistent until after Christmas (the ASIN mentioned is for the new set that replaced the old model, which is no longer carried on Amazon).

Here is the link to the post:
https://www.facebook.com/groups/scanpower/permalink/304336013001665/

You must be a member of the ScanPower Facebook group to read this post. If you are not a member, I highly recommend joining!

Chapter 5 – The Scanner Monkey Way

"It is the mission of the Scanner Monkey group to provide a positive, uplifting and fun place in which online sellers can gather and share BOLOs and retail arbitrage tips with other like-minded and positive thinking members without fear of persecution or negativity."

Jay Bayne
Scanner Monkey Founder

The Scanner Monkey Mission Statement shown above was first posted in our Facebook group on November 18, 2013, as a friendly reminder of why we were all part of the Scanner Monkey tribe. This was my vision for the group and it was my hope that every member would be comforted to know that they could freely share information for the benefit of all with no fear of negativity. I'll admit it's a bit wordy, and using the term "persecution" may sound like we are avoiding a witch hunt, but that was that was the environment we were dealing with at the time. I wanted everyone to feel safe from the naysayers and negative nellies that were more prevalent at the time. In essence, I wanted the Scanner Monkey tribe to feel like it was in its own safe little gated community (I guess that makes me the "Neighborhood Watch Captain").

By the way, you may notice that I use the word "tribe" quite a bit when talking about the Scanner Monkey community. It seems appropriate given that a group of monkeys is often called a "tribe." Also, dictionary.com defines a tribe as "any aggregate

of people united by ties of [...] customs and traditions, etc."
Scanner Monkey tribe members are clearly united by certain
customs, traditions, and common behaviors.

There is a certain behavior that is prevalent within a tribe of
Scanner Monkeys. Actually, behavior may not be the best term
because, let's be honest, half the fun of Scanner Monkey is a
little fun *mis*behavior. **We like to joke around and have more
fun than a barrel of monkeys!**

Instead of "behavior," we prefer to call it the "Scanner Monkey
Way." This code of conduct is evidenced by the posts that are
shared daily within the Scanner Monkey group.

The Scanner Monkey Way

A Scanner Monkey:

- Shares information for the benefit of the entire tribe.
- Reciprocates and give as much as they receive.
- Congratulates others on their successes.
- Commiserates with others over their hardships.
- Practices "co-opetition" over competition (see Scanner Monkey Lingo for definitions).
- Respects fellow sellers and would never knowingly do anything to harm their businesses.
- Hunts for profitable products and believes it to be one of the greatest joys in the world!
- Enjoys sourcing with other Scanner Monkeys in their area.
- Believes in the "abundance mentality" – there is plenty of profitable inventory for everyone to sell.
- Appreciates the veterans within the group, as well as contributions made by newbies.

The Scanner Monkey Way

🍌 Enjoys what they do...unless you are talking about packing and shipping (ugh).

🍌 Appreciates different types of business models.

🍌 Believes that what goes around comes around (some call it karma or kismet).

🍌 Knows that two heads are better than one...and 200 heads are better than two...and so on and so on.

🍌 Motivates others to succeed.

🍌 Thinks that BOLOs are cool!

🍌 Celebrates their Scanner Monkey PRIDE!

Scanner Monkeys Showing Their Scanner Monkey Pride!

The Scanner Monkey Way

The Scanner Monkey Way isn't the only way to approach the wonderful world of online selling, but I firmly believe it is the best way! I don't expect everyone to agree, but I know that the Scanner Monkeys do.

Chapter 6 – BOLO-ology

"Many were afraid that group BOLOs would mean that the prices on those items would plummet BUT - that has not been the case. We're all makin' money at Scanner Monkey"

Marlo McCarthy
Scanner Monkey

A BOLO is an item or type of item to lookout for. It should be found at a low enough price that selling it on Amazon or eBay is profitable. The most important factor that all Scanner Monkey BOLOs have in common is that they are **crowd sourced**. Within the Scanner Monkey group we are able to share the benefits of many perspectives, many levels of experience, many locations, many budgets, and many types of shoppers.

When you discuss sharing BOLOs for the benefit of an entire group of online sellers, the best place to start is what **type** of BOLOs you should be sharing.

There are several different key types of BOLOs that we'll discuss below:

The RARE BOLO or HTF BOLO: Free Money!

The rare BOLO is sometimes called a "true" BOLO because you really have to "look out for" this item because it is **truly** hard to find (HTF). It is **not** on endcaps at every Walmart across the country. It is **not** an advertised item in the weekly Toys R Us circular. These items are HTF because there may only be a few in the stores. Some examples of the rare BOLO include:

- Clearance items – Not every store within a chain has the same products on clearance, so it may be harder to find in other areas.
- Seasonal items – Halloween candies that sell year round or Christmas themed products.
- Short packs - Some manufacturers only produce a small amount of one particular doll or action figure in the line. (i.e. there is only one of this character in a box of 12).
- Discontinued or out of production items - An item might still be found in stores even though the manufacturer may have discontinued the item.
- Regional products – These are items that are only carried at certain stores or chains within a geographic area.
- "Exclusively at Store" items – These are items that are carried only in specific stores. An example would be certain private labeled grocery items carried only in HEB stores in Texas.

These true BOLOs are popular (i.e. with a low Amazon ranking) and hard to find, so high demand, combined with a limited supply, drives the price up.

When you find one of these true BOLOs, you must always check the **current** Amazon price to make sure that the item is still profitable, but if so, buy buy buy!

Here are a few examples:

- A discontinued women's facial cream is on clearance at Marshalls. It is marked down to $4 a tub and sells for $40 on Amazon. There are women all over the country who love this cream and want to buy it even though the company has decided to discontinue it. They will pay a premium. One seller has checked every Marshalls in her area and bought eight of the item. There are no more to be found in her area. She then posts it in the Scanner Monkey Facebook group and in the BOLOG so that sellers in other places can look for this cream at their Marshalls too. Since it is in limited supply, even if 2,000 people went to their local Marshalls, bought every tub of this cream they could find, and sent them all in to Amazon, the demand would still be high.

🍌 A Halloween/Evil Disney Queen themed make up kit is hidden in the cosmetics section of Walgreens. It does not even come close to selling out for Halloween and is quickly marked down post-holiday to rock bottom prices. It is still very popular online. Once again the demand far outweighs the supply of clearance items at Walgreens, and it is not being produced any more. This BOLO is shared on the group, and the members that locate it can make a nice profit from it.

While these BOLOs can be extremely profitable, they are **rare** which means that many sellers will not be able to locate the specific item. However, the sellers can use this as information to determine what **types** of items to scan and which **new sections** of stores to scan in. These BOLOs are valuable both when found exactly as listed and for the lessons they can teach us about other similar profitable items.

The Unfound RARE BOLO: Your Treasure Map!

Unfound BOLOs are like a pirate's treasure map. If a seller cannot find the exact BOLO that is shared, it still marks a big X on the treasure map. While it may be frustrating that there is not an exact map to every hidden gem, a buyer can still look in the **area** of that BOLO and sometimes find a different treasure.

Say, for instance, that a Scanner Monkey member is looking for a Sunbeam Dog Treat Maker that he saw shared in the group. This particular product can be purchased for $20 at Petco and will "fetch" $85 on Amazon (pun intended). The member searches high and low, but is unable to locate that exact make and model in the store. He does, however, find a Chillin' Bonz Frozen Small Dog Puppy Treat Maker that he buys for $10 in the store and resells for $35 on Amazon. Although he didn't find what he was originally looking for, he opened up his eyes to a new type of product and found another profitable item that he can add to his list of BOLOs for future reference!

This could very well be the most valuable aspect of sharing BOLOs with a group like Scanner Monkey. It's not always about finding the exact product that was shared, but rather honing your sourcing skills to locate other profitable products in areas you would not have ordinarily searched in. Essentially, it's the difference between **handing** someone a fish and **teaching** them how to fish. We may all have moments and days when we are hungry and just want some fish! But, in the long run, knowing **how to find** the fish or find hidden treasure will pay off more than if the original item had been found.

Use BOLOs both RARE and UNFOUND to be your SOURCING TREASURE MAP!

Remember, the key to the success of both of the previous types of BOLOs is their rarity. If they are truly a HTF BOLO, then sharing them with hundreds or even thousands of other sellers in a group will not seriously impact demand or price. For a full discussion of this, along with supporting data, see Al Craig and

Brian Bly's book, *The Truth about Retail Arbitrage BOLO's and their effect on the market place.* This book is available on Amazon at: www.amazon.com/Truth-Retail-Arbitrage-effect-market/dp/1497448131/

The ACTIONABLE BOLO

The actionable BOLO is an item that is in many stores, will sell for a good profit online, and is simply not known by everyone. One buyer has found a particular toy or grocery item that sells well consistently, and he is the only or one of few sellers of this item currently. He may not want to share this easy to find item with hundreds of other sellers, but is willing to share it with one or two friends, especially knowing that his buddies will return the favor.

An Example of an Actionable BOLO (fictional but based on a true story):

A certain reseller knows that Walmart carries Java Junky coffee in a 24 oz bag for $3.99 regularly. It sells on Amazon for about $17.99 per bag and is ranked 45,673 with three other Prime sellers. On average this means about five of these items sell per week. The reseller tells a friend about it, and in return she tells him about Cleanee Soap, which is sold as a three pack at Walmart for $2.99 and sells online for $19.99. They both learn about one more thing they can buy at Walmart and eventually fall in love and get married. They have a monkey themed wedding and do not pay full price for anything. (Ok, I may have gotten carried away there, but you get the idea.)

The Scanner Monkey Way

How Does Scanner Monkey Help You Profit from these BOLOs?

- 🍌 Scanner Monkey Facebook Group - members post RARE BOLOs daily and also answer questions about how to find more good items to buy and sell.
- 🍌 The BOLO Exchange Facebook Group – a place where people can privately exchange ACTIONABLE BOLOs to provide and receive value. Friendships can be formed. Dare we say love? Bromance? BFFs?
- 🍌 BOLOG (aka "BOLO blog") – this is our members only, web based database of deals. All of the RARE BOLOs from the Facebook group are compiled into this resource, which can be accessed on the go or at home. It is sortable by store or product category.

All of these resources are covered in greater detail in the next chapters.

In conclusion, the prolonged study and practice of BOLO-OLOGY will result in smarter, happier, and wealthier sellers. A useful pursuit!

Chapter 7 – Scanner Monkey Resources Overview

"It's a jungle out there and this is a great place to hang out with our fellow entrepreneurs and get recharged! There are lots of BOLOs for our 'monkey business' and generous people who will reveal their BOLOs and cheer you on when you score one! MONKEY ON!"

Terry Menig
Scanner Monkey Member

As the Scanner Monkey Facebook group continues to grow and evolve, so do the services we offer. We do offer services to the online seller community as a whole, as well as exclusive services for our paid members.

Scanner Monkey Facebook group

The Facebook group is where it all began and where most Scanner Monkeys still spend a majority of their time. It's the Scanner Monkey jungle where the monkeys can gather in real time to share tips, talk about their successes, swap stories, crack a few jokes, and discuss gathering those sweet BOLO bananas.

It is a fast paced and dynamic community that is for members only. There are frequently over 30 individual posts per day - some informational, some BOLOs, some fun, some asking for help, and some sharing resources.

The content on the Facebook page is so valuable that we started a page on our website to log the best conversations for later reference (ScannerMonkey.com → Member Resources → Facebook Hot Links).

The Scanner Monkey Way

You can find the Scanner Monkey Facebook group here: https://www.facebook.com/groups/scannermonkey/

ScannerMonkey.com

The website furthers the mission of sharing resources. There is a section of the website with learning resources for the public as well as those that are for members only. We offer information about useful books, free videos, podcasts, and more. We share information about other groups as well. Essentially, ScannerMonkey.com is an information hub for the online selling community.

Community Resources (that means FREE):

- SMTV (**S**canner **M**onkey **TV**) – A weekly show that is available live online or in replay that includes interviews with experts that share tips and strategies that can be implemented today.
- Recommended books, apps, and websites for beginners and beyond. These are the best of the best and a central place to find out what to read/see/use to grow your online selling business.
- A calendar of podcasts and shows that are put on by the many members of the online seller community (not just the Scanner Monkeys).

Members Only Resources:
- The BOLOG – our online product find database (it's a BOLO BLOG!)
- Member Discounts – members only discounts for FBA products and services (save $100s!)
- Facebook Hot Links – an archive of the best posts from the Facebook group

The BOLOG

The BOLOG is the directory of BOLOs that have been crowd sourced by members. All the BOLOs that are reported in the Facebook group are transferred to the BOLOG for easy reference.

Members use the BOLOG to see what other sellers have found by store or category. It can be accessed on the ScannerMonkey.com website from internet enabled phones and other mobile devices, as well as computers.

There are a few different ways to use this amazing resource. One is to simply look for the exact same item that another buyer found and see if it is available in your area. If it is not, a buyer can use the BOLOG to get ideas on new areas of stores and new types of products to source. If an item is hard to find in a brick and mortar store, then members can search for those items in online stores to see if they are available there.

The BOLO Exchange Facebook Group

A brain child of Chris Green, the BOLO Exchange is where Scanner Monkey members can go to post, trade, and exchange BOLO's **privately** and for mutual benefit.

It is a place to connect with individual members to exchange specific and actionable items to expand both parties' offerings. Participation is voluntary, and like so many in things in life, those who can participate more heavily will receive more value. You must be a Scanner Monkey member to join this group.

You can find the BOLO Exchange by going here:
https://www.facebook.com/groups/BoloExchange/

The Scanner Monkey Way

Scanner Monkey TV (SMTV)

Each week Scanner Monkeys Jay Bayne and Cordelia Blake host an online, educational show. They interview a variety of experts and sellers and have covered such topics as:

- Online arbitrage
- Buying and selling groceries
- Estate sales/thrifting
- Creating effective Amazon listings
- Action figures
- Wholesale sourcing
- Analysis tools
- Taking a paycheck and growing AZ business
- Accounting basics of business setup
- Delegating and hiring virtual assistants
- More...

These episodes are all available to the FBA community. The shows are on http://Spreecast.com/users/ScannerMonkey each Thursday night at 9pm (Eastern Standard Time) or can be watched on replay at any time. For a full list of shows you can go to: http://scannermonkey.com/resources/scanner-monkey-tv .

As you can see, there is something for everyone at Scanner Monkey. Do you have a question about which Bluetooth scanner is the best, or you want to talk about your first $1,000/day in sales on Amazon? Share it in the Facebook group. Do you want to privately exchange an actionable BOLO with another Scanner Monkey member? Check out the BOLO Exchange Facebook group. Or perhaps you want to access hundreds of archived BOLOs on your smart phone while sourcing in your local Walmart? Check out our BOLOG on the ScannerMonkey.com website.

These are the resources that will "help you make more money and have more fun" (catchy title, right?). One tip, one link, or one idea could add hundreds or even thousands of dollars to your bottom line each month. And you get all of the aforementioned tools for only $9.99/month or $99/yr for membership to the group.

The following chapters will give you greater detail on each of these services and walk you through how to best utilize each one.

Chapter 8 – Scanner Monkey Facebook Group

"Surround yourself with the dreamers and the doers, the believers and the thinkers, but most of all, surround yourself with those who see greatness within you, even when you don't see it yourself."

Edmund Lee
Author

The "Scanner Monkey Revolution" first entered the public consciousness in October 2013 with the formation of the Facebook group. The Facebook group preceded everything else related to Scanner Monkey. At this time there was no website, no BOLOG, no BOLO Exchange, no book….just a Facebook group of positive minded sellers.

It all started with one admin (me, Jay), two members (Chris Green and Brian Vienneau), and the following post: "Welcome to Scanner Monkey, where we can share retail arbitrage tips, funny stories and **maybe** even share a few BOLOs." I emphasize the word "maybe" in this sentence because I was just dangling the idea of sharing BOLOs in a group setting. This whole thing could have blown up in my face if a majority of the members didn't want to share their BOLOs with other members.

It turned out that the first Scanner Monkey members went so bananas about openly sharing that BOLOs comprised a majority of the early posts. I can still remember the very first BOLO. It was a Braun Active Ion Hairbrush shared by one of the first members of Scanner Monkey, Duane Malek (he also runs a great Facebook group called Fast Turn Radio).

First Scanner Monkey BOLO

10/30/13

Found at TJ Maxx for $10

Sold on Amazon for $50

Thanks Duane Malek!

The BOLOs just spiraled on from there. Members wanted to share their finds and learn about new ones. Since then we have shared hundreds of BOLOs! However, that is far from the only benefit in our little barrel of monkeys. Members also come to hang out, share online selling tips, ask questions, answer questions, tell stories, crack jokes, show sourcing photos, share successes, and so much more.

I may be a little biased, but I truly feel like it is one of the best online selling communities on Facebook. We are a tight-knit bunch, and the members are very engaged in the discussions. Members may join for the BOLOs, but they stay for the camaraderie.

The Scanner Monkey Way

Here are just a FEW of the topics we've discussed in detail on our Facebook group:

- Best portable scanners
- Creating multi packs and bundles
- How different sellers got to where they are (over 10K, 100K, 1 mil etc...)
- Best apps, books & websites
- How to edit photos
- Experts discuss their niches
- How to use Evernote
- Online arbitrage
- Health and Beauty
- Best stuff to stock up on after Christmas
- Sourcing and shipping on the road
- Repricers
- Starting with a small budget
- Wholesale info
- What's your daily routine?

The great thing is that even if you joined after these conversations occurred, you can easily click back and either peruse for info or even bump the post up to the top and get the conversation started again.

As I mentioned in "The Scanner Monkey Way" chapter, Scanner Monkeys want to make money, but they also want to have fun! Personally, I don't want to do something unless I can have fun while doing it...so it's important to me that my group has some fun too! Yes, there are serious discussions about topics that can help you move your business forward, but there are also funny stories, contests, and merchandise giveaways to keep things entertaining (see below for a couple of my favorites).

Caption This Contest

EBAY PRODUCT LISTING

OR CRAIGSLIST PERSONAL AD?

"Raindog Deals" was nice enough to let us use one his eBay listing pictures for this contest. Can you guess what he was selling? The Shoes! Winner received an action figure that was selling on Amazon for about $65.

BOLO Contest

DON'T KEEP CALM
BECAUSE IT'S
CONTEST TIME!

Members submitted their BOLOs and the one with the highest dollar profit received a $100 Gift card from Amazon.

Thoughtful Posts

Steven
December 11, 2013 · Waynesville, MO

I have blown up in sales over these past 7 days. I'm fresh out of high school and attending college, just started doing FBA 3 months ago! My goal for this month was 4k in sales but I have already broken 10! I'm so thankful for having a great group of monkeys that keep me motivated with their stories!!! Hope I can keep these numbers after Q4

	Ordered product sales	Units
7 Days	$8,902.82	132
15 Days	$9,410.28	156
30 Days	$10,694.08	242

View more of your sales statistics

Unlike Comment

👍 You, Cordelia Blake, Karin Isgur Bergsagel, Matt Carlett and 67 others like this.

Jennifer   That is so great, Steven!! Wow!!! Have you been selling mostly toys? Keep it up 😊
December 11, 2013 at 5:43am · Like

Paula   fantastic job! Happy for you!
December 11, 2013 at 5:48am · Like

Laura   Congratulations Steven!
December 11, 2013 at 5:58am · Like

Niurka   Woot woot!! You're awesome!! Keep at it and those numbers will multiply!!! 😊
December 11, 2013 at 6:38am · Like

Karin
April 1 · Williamsburg, VA

#monkeysmademedoit I met and exceeded my Q1 goal, which was $1K/day in gross sales. In fact, I have just had my first 6-figure quarter, outside Q4. Best part? My sales are up 77% over the same period last year, but my total items sold are only up 50%. That represents a 17% increase in ASP (average selling price). I have gone from $29 to $32. And that is despite selling a boatload of Valentine's cards, which brought the average down.

Now, I know as well as anyone that if you don't know all the numbers, you really don't know any numbers, but I'm still not willing to completely open my books on that in a large group 😊 Let's just say that I am very happy with what I am banking, too.

About the hashtag? TRUE. ScannerMonkey is in large part responsible for this growth. And it wasn't the bolo's that got me here, folks. It was the tribe spirit - the honest sharing, the real examples, the amazing work ethics, the generous spirit, the accept-no-limitations thinking - that completely rocked my world. The then prevailing negativity had nearly dragged me under. I didn't realize what a gray and stale world I was living in until SM drew the curtains, opened the windows, and let in fresh air and sunlight.

I won't name individuals - there are too many, and I'd hate to miss a name - but thank you all.

Attitude won't fix everything, but it sure does help.

Unlike · Comment

👍 You, Cordelia Blake, Chris Green, Duane Malek and 158 others like this.

💬 View previous comments   50 of 72

Teresa   Congratulations on a very impressive feat! When KIB comments, I read. Thanks for sharing your awesomeness!
April 1 at 9:00am · Edited · Unlike · 👍 7

Peter   Well said! Congrats!
April 1 at 9:27am · Like · 👍 1

As you can see from these posts the members genuinely care about each other and want to help each other out whenever possible. They may sell against each other, but because they have an abundance mentality, they know that the Amazon pie is so huge that everyone can have a big slice.

Although helping each other out is the primary reason for many Facebook groups, we give more by recruiting and getting to know the FBA experts, coaches, and vendors within the group. In fact, we have a spreadsheet in our files section with information on more than 60 member experts and vendors in the world of online selling. These are Scanner Monkey members that have agreed to allow other group members to message them privately if they have any questions relating to their area of expertise.

Here's just a small sampling of some of our Scanner Monkey member experts (watch your toes, we are about to drop some big names): Chris Green, Jim Cockrum, Duane Malek, Jessica Larrew, Brad DeGraw, Bob Willey, Cynthia Stine, Matt Carlett, Stephen Smotherman, Skip McGrath, Amanda Moak, and many other coaches, writers, and Facebook group leaders.

Keep in mind that just because these particular member experts are well known for their coaching courses or books doesn't mean that they are the **only** member experts. We have several other members that happen to be experts in various fields related to online selling - members who specialize in selling health and personal care, selling on eBay, online arbitrage, selling while taking care of kids, traveltage, and a multitude of other topics. We interview many of these members on our weekly Scanner Monkey TV shows (more on that in Chapter 12).

We also have vendors in the group that are available to answer any questions a member may have about FBA related services that they use or are considering. Some examples include: Mark LeVine from Bubble Fast shipping supplies, Christie Carbone from Serialio ScanFob (we are, after all, SCANNER monkeys), Mark Faggiano from Tax Jar, Chris Green from ScanPower, Izabella DeSouza from App Eagle repricer, Ryan Stephens from Inventory Lab, and many others. This means that Scanner Monkey is a one stop shop and customer service department for many FBA related services.

It may sound cliché, but I truly believe that our members are THE most valuable resource in Scanner Monkey. My dad used to always tell me to "surround yourself with people that are smarter than you." I think he would be very pleased to see that I am taking his advice with the talent that is assembled within the Scanner Monkey group. And when I say talent, I'm including the newbies in that group as well. Many of the newbies share valuable advice right alongside the veterans of the group. The newbies inspire me just as much as the million dollar sellers because many times they can accomplish as much in their first six months as some veterans did in six years!

The Scanner Monkey Facebook group helps us to celebrate and learn from ALL online sellers...and one way it shows is every time a member lets us peek behind the curtains at their sales history:

The Scanner Monkey Way

Catherine   ► **ScannerMonkey**
June 12   TX 🖫

I really want to thank everyone in this group. I am brand new to FBA. My first shipment was received just last month. I posted here on May 13th that I got my first sale. I had been reading anything I ran across and listened to dozen of podcasts and watched spreecasts and YouTube videos. (Some guy on a cruise ship filming made me SO jealous! lol)

When I was listening to a Thrifting for Profit podcast, they were going on and on and on and on about SM. I joined for a month and quickly realized I was hooked and would subscribe for a year. Megan posts AZ to AZ and I tried one as a complete newbie and it was a huge success! When a BOLO is posted, I will google the product and try to purchase some if the price is right. My son went to Paris and I went to 6 different Barnes and Noble Bookstores for another BOLO. I have found a lot of clearance stuff, purchased TONS of toys in anticipation for Q4 and tested several replens (and have 5-6 I feel will bring in $200/mo each). As many of you may know (I mention it, but won't dwell on it), my husband and I (still honeymooners) are heart patients. I heard @ Jessica Larrew on Pat Flynn's podcast, told my husband I wanted to do this, and the rest is right here in front of me. (NOT history!) Here are my first 30 days' stats. This past week is when my test replens hit the FC and sales went crazy! Sending more in today.

THANK YOU ALL AGAIN!!!!!!

👍 You, Duane Malek, Brian Vienneau, Karin Isgur Bergsagel and 69 others like this.

Jessica   Good job!
June 12 at 11:00am · Like · 👍1

Jennifer   Awesome job!!!!!!!
June 12 at 11:13am · Like · 👍1

Reid   Wow!
June 12 at 11:39am · Like · 👍1

Kelly Jo   Woop Woop! Awesome work
June 12 at 11:43am · Like · 👍1

Jim   Way to go! Keep up the great work. 🙂
June 12 at 11:51am · Like · 👍1

Peggy   that is an awesome start! Especially this time of the year! Great job!
June 12 at 12:49pm · Like · 👍1

Kevin   Looking good
June 12 at 1:07pm · Like · 👍1

Megan   Congrats Catherine!
June 12 at 1:26pm · Like · 👍1

Robert   Great stuff Catherine!
June 12 at 2:24pm · Like · 👍1

The Scanner Monkey Way

You can see from this post that our members really do support each other with virtual high fives and pats on backs. In fact, there have even been some Scanner Monkey meet ups to help each other source.

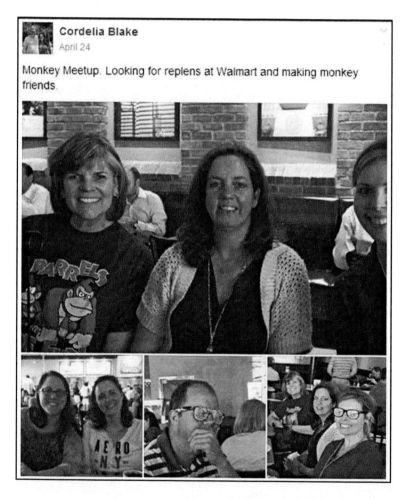

The Facebook group has led to group meetups in person as well as many friendships. It gives those who want a chance to connect and exchange ideas and fun.

The Scanner Monkey Way

We do have members who are not fans of Facebook and choose to simply interact with the BOLOG on the website. Some create Facebook profiles simply for the purpose of navigating the online selling community, including Scanner Monkey. There are so many ways to participate and grow.

I could fill another entire book with stories and photos of our members (sequel?). If you want to see more, then head over to our website and join our Facebook group.

Chapter 9 – ScannerMonkey.com

"Just wanted you to know the new web site is really great. You guys have done an awesome job on providing so much valuable information for the Amazon (or even an eBay) seller."

Vickie Stewart
Scanner Monkey Member

When this group originally started, BOLOs were simply posted on the Facebook group by enthusiastic members, and that was it. There was no organized way for someone to compile them in a list when out shopping. Several members came up with their own solutions, from copying them to a spreadsheet, to organizing them in phone photo albums, to uploading them into Evernote. It was evident that Jay needed to find a simpler way to create an easy to search BOLO list which could be accessed **securely** by the members.

This is when Jay and I (Cordelia) started working together to come up with a solution. What started as a conversation about BOLOs, turned into something much greater (as so many BOLO conversations do). As Rick said in *Casablanca*, it was "the beginning of a beautiful friendship."

We initially put together an easily accessible database to manage access to the BOLOs using a simple blogging platform called Blogspot. My 11 year old son, Alexander, heard about the project and said, "You should call it the BOLOG. A Bolo Blog!" His term stuck and is used routinely every day.

The Scanner Monkey Way

As time went on, it became clear that a hub for information beyond just a Facebook group would be helpful. We could offer additional resources to our members as well as provide information about how non-members could join. Facebook is a wonderful tool but lacks many features. So we started to plan and design our website to provide a hub of resources for the Scanner Monkey group. Based on the recommendation of FBA coach Jessica Larrew, we decided to hire Cindy Bidar, a web developer that specializes in creating membership sites. Below is a screenshot of our creation, ScannerMonkey.com [1.0 version]:

We wanted a balance of information about joining, testimonials, and resources. We collaborated with Cindy for a couple of months during the design and build out phase, and the website went live on February 3, 2014.

We have resources such as SMTV (Scanner Monkey TV), recommended websites, apps, and books that are available to non-members. There are also member photos, information about the Scanner Monkey team, and more.

The Scanner Monkey Way

Each member has a unique login to the site and can access all of the following resources:

- The BOLOG
- Member resources
- Exclusive discounts
- Archives of all past SMTV shows – a big storehouse of knowledge
- Facebook Hot Links page with links to useful and entertaining posts from the group
- Audio versions of our SMTV shows for easy listening

The formation of the website helped us to solidify our mission and gave us a platform to provide new resources as often as possible.

The testimonial section is inspirational for new and old members. In so many different ways, the Scanner Monkey group has impacted lives, transformed business models, and helped people. It is very rewarding to be a part of a group that has helped so many people. When we are so busy all the time, it is easy to forget how much impact helping another person can have.

Chapter 10 – The BOLOG = BOLO Blog

"I used the BOLOG at CVS, and in less than 30 minutes I had found 38 Beanie Babies that were selling anywhere from $25 to $69 each!!! Wow, unbelievable.....this one trip to CVS had already paid off 10 times more than my subscription cost to ScannerMonkey.com!"

Michele Pearls
Scanner Monkey Member

Even though the BOLOG is part of ScannerMonkey.com, it is such an important component of the group that it warrants its own chapter. It's an integral part of why many members join Scanner Monkey in the first place.

Hanging out with other Scanner Monkeys in the Facebook group can be both educational and entertaining (some would call it "edutainment"). But, like many Facebook groups, it can also be a bit of a time suck if you're not careful. If you want to bypass the tips, questions, conversations, and jokes whizzing by in the group and get straight to the profitable product finds, then the BOLOG is where you want to be. The BOLOG allows you get in, get BOLOs, and get out lickety-split.

The BOLOG was created to provide a centralized place to house all the BOLOs that are crowd sourced by the Scanner Monkey members. It can only be accessed on the ScannerMonkey.com website with a member's log in.

Here is how the BOLOG works:

1) A Scanner Monkey member finds a profitable product to resell on Amazon and starts a post with "#BOLO" or "BOLO" in the Facebook group. The BOLO post should include the store name where the product was found, the price paid for the product, and the Amazon link with price at time of posting (ATOP).

2) The staff at Scanner Monkey will upload all of the BOLO information to the BOLOG on ScannerMonkey.com.

Imodium Multi-Symptom Relief of Diarrhea, Mint, 42-Count Chewable Tablets

NOVEMBER 7, 2013 BY **CORDELIA** — LEAVE A COMMENT

Paid $11

http://www.amazon.com/Imodium-Multi-Symptom-Diarrhea-42-Count-Chewable/dp/B001CCUBX6/ref=sr_1_1?s=hpc&ie=UTF8&qid=1383767327&sr=1-1&keywords=imodium+chewables

3) Members view the BOLOG and search for products by store or product category. We have even included a search box so you can look for specific products while at your store (ex: search for "Transformers"). This can be done on your laptop or on your smart phone while you are in the store sourcing.

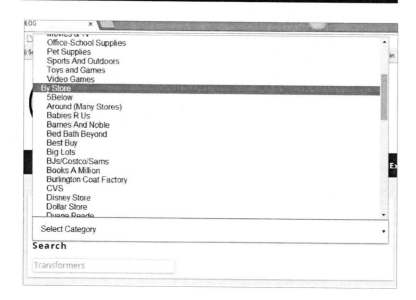

The BOLOG is updated at least every 48 hours with the latest product finds that were sourced by the Scanner Monkey members.

For a video tutorial on how to use the BOLOG go here: http://www.youtube.com/watch?v=CjefGMaMmXs

It's important to note that the BOLOs shared on the BOLOG are typically items that are harder to find, seasonal, or clearance items. For more actionable BOLOs (see BOLO-ology chapter) that you don't want to share with hundreds of other members, I recommend that you use the BOLO Exchange Facebook group, covered in the next chapter.

Chapter 11 – The BOLO Exchange Facebook Group

"I really like the group so far. I've made a few exchanges, scored a couple of good BOLOS, made some new friends, and hopefully shared something worthwhile."

David Penley

BOLO Exchange Member

I would love to take all the credit for the BOLO Exchange, because I think it's a fantastic idea. Alas, I cannot because the BOLO Exchange was originally conceptualized by Chris Green. Believe it or not, it all started because he "was being lazy" (his words...not mine).

Chris has always said that "easy always wins" so when Chris wanted a couple of BOLOs he took the easy road and just posted a request in the Facebook groups, rather than looking them up on the BOLOG. He would go to the Scan Power or Scanner Monkey Facebook group and post "I'm going to Toys R Us...hit me up with a couple of BOLOs." Of course not everyone can get away with that! However, when the "Godfather of Retail Arbitrage" makes a request, his followers are happy to oblige...including me.

The Scanner Monkey Way

Because Chris Green lives by the "Scanner Monkey Way," he will happily swap one of his own BOLOs for a BOLO that he receives from another Scanner Monkey or Scan Power member. After doing this a couple of times he wondered if there was a way to scale this BOLO trading. Cue the light bulb! Chris called me and said, "Let's start a BOLO exchange!" I remember replying "A BOLO *what*?"

Once Chris explained the basic premise of exchanging BOLOs **privately** with each other, I thought it was another "powerful idea whose time had come." Coincidentally, it also provided a solution to a problem that we were having with Scanner Monkey at the time. Our members were nervous about sharing certain **actionable** BOLOs because they were afraid that once they posted to 1000+ members, then the prices would tank. Note that I emphasized the word "actionable," because if you post a true hard-to-find BOLO, it really shouldn't matter if the membership is 1000, 2000, or even 5000.

After we discussed how the BOLOs would be exchanged, Chris and I created The BOLO Exchange Facebook group on April 5, 2014, and gave the Scanner Monkeys exclusive rights to the group. It just made sense to incorporate this group within Scanner Monkey because it was already known for sharing BOLOs on a large scale. This just offered another avenue to network with other members to share BOLOs privately. The first admins in the group were Chris Green, Duane Malek, and Jay Bayne. Currently, the admins are Jay Bayne and Cordelia Blake, and the group is 100% a part of Scanner Monkey.

The Scanner Monkey Way

Now we just needed to explain this foreign concept to the Scanner Monkey members. We created a tutorial video that explained how to privately share BOLOs with select members within the group. This video can be found at: http://scannermonkey.com/boloexchange/

The trades are posted by members in the BOLO Exchange using the following format: ""I have a BOLO from ___ store, ranked around ____, and will return $___ in profit. I will swap for a BOLO from ___ store."" Or, the member could just request *any* BOLO with similar profit.

A BOLO Exchange post

Once again the gas for this engine is **reciprocity**. People often say "it's better to give than receive." With the BOLO Exchange you can do **both** and both parties benefit!

On the surface the benefit is obvious – you receive a new BOLO in return for your BOLO. However, it goes deeper than that. There are several other benefits to utilizing this group:

- You develop stronger and more intimate relationships with other Scanner Monkeys that have complementary business models.
- By networking with other members of the BOLO Exchange you could develop your own more focused mastermind groups.
- Not only can you exchange actionable BOLOs, but you could also exchange replens (replenishable items) with other members.
- You can exchange a wider variety of BOLOs than you could in the Scanner Monkey group with as many or as few members as you wish. Some members may choose to exchange with one other member or they could exchange with five other members. You have greater control over your actionable BOLO.

The Scanner Monkey Way

Clearly BOLOs have value. The BOLO Exchange helps you get the most of that value. You can trade or share on YOUR terms. You can meet people and create context with them. You can build win-win relationships. The bottom line is you GIVE value and you GET value.

So, if you are a Scanner Monkey then joining the BOLO Exchange is as simple as clicking "Join Group" on this page: https://www.facebook.com/groups/BoloExchange/

If you are not a Scanner Monkey, then you would need to join Scanner Monkey first in order to take advantage of this networking group for exchanging BOLOs.

The Scanner Monkey Way

Chapter 12 – Scanner Monkey TV (SMTV)

"Each SMTV episode contains informative, educational, inspirational, and often hilarious interviews with other Scanner Monkeys who are finding success."

Stephen Smotherman
Scanner Monkey Member

At Scanner Monkey, we are always looking for new ways to learn and share helpful information. We started our weekly internet TV show in late December of 2013 to provide a platform for members to interact with each other. We currently use Spreecast.com because it is free for viewers, relatively easy to use, and includes a live chat for audience interaction. The live chat is an integral part of Scanner Monkey TV because it allows our members to ask the guests and moderators questions about the topic of discussion.

SMTV Episode with Jason T. Smith

The Scanner Monkey Way

The show has had over 20 guests at the time of writing this book. We have learned from sellers who sell over 1 million dollars per year in product, part time sellers who make over 200K, and many more. Here is a sampling of the topics of our shows:

- How Scanner Monkey started
- Online arbitrage
- Selling groceries online
- Estate sales/thrifting
- Creating effective Amazon listings
- Buying and selling action figures
- Wholesale sourcing
- Analysis tools
- Taking a paycheck and growing AZ business
- Accounting basics and business setup
- Delegating and hiring virtual assistants
- Interviews with power sellers

The latest show is available for free to the community. Only members have access to the full archives. Shows are broadcast live every Thursday at 9pm Eastern Standard Time and can be viewed live for full participation or later as a replay. We have an active chat during the show as well as live give-aways. For a full list of shows, please see our website:

http://scannermonkey.com/resources/scanner-monkey-tv/

The Scanner Monkey Way

Chapter 13 – Scanner Monkey Lingo

If you are new to selling online, you may not be familiar with all of the words, terms, and acronyms used by Scanner Monkeys and most online sellers. It's our Scanner Monkey lingo!

Abundance Mentality
1) Believing there is plenty for everyone.
2) The abiding belief held by Scanner Monkeys that governs their need to share in their good fortune with others.

Arbitrage - The financial practice of taking advantage of a price difference between two or more markets.

BOLO – Be On Look Out for products, generally hard to find, that are available in retail stores or online and can be resold for a profit.

BOLO Monkey
1) Scanner Monkey mascot.
2) Any monkey action figure or doll that can be posed next to a BOLO to illustrate that a Scanner Monkey found that product!
3) A BOLO monkey loves the limelight and can be seen in several pictures on the Facebook group.
4) Considered by many Scanner Monkeys to be a good luck charm.

Consumable - A product that needs to be replaced by customers on a routine basis, such as toothpaste, shampoo, groceries, etc.

Co-opetition – A business strategy based on a combination of cooperation and competition, derived from an understanding that business competitors (i.e. Amazon online sellers) can benefit when they work together.

Crowd sourcing – Information gathered from within a large group of people and then shared for the benefit of everyone in the group.

Fast nickel – A product that sells quickly online, but returns a smaller profit margin.

Fast Turn Inventory – Inventory that "turns" (sells) quickly. Many times these are consumable items that are purchased repeatedly like toothpaste, shampoo, groceries, etc…

Long tail products – Unique and harder to find products with relatively small quantities sold of each. The long tail was popularized by author, Chris Anderson, in an October 2004 "Wired" magazine article. See also *Slow Dime*.

Long Term Hold – Buying inventory with the intent of storing it for several months to sell later at a higher price.

The Scanner Monkey Way

Online Arbitrage – The practice of buying products on one market online to sell at a different market online at a profit.

Prime Seller – A third party seller on Amazon that utilizes the FBA program to attract buyers that are interested in fast two day shipping and Amazon's liberal return policy.

Reciprocity – The practice of exchanging things and ideas with others for mutual benefit.

Replen (or Replenishable) - An item that can be purchased repeatedly from a known source at a consistent price.

Retail Arbitrage - The practice of buying items in a retail location at a discounted price and selling them for more online.

Scanner Monkey

1) Someone who goes bananas for buying products at retail stores or online and reselling on Amazon or other online selling platforms.

2) A person who embraces technology - using scanners, smart phones, computers, and tablets to locate profitable products to sell online.

3) An online seller who is constantly learning and growing his or her business with other members of the Scanner Monkey tribe.

4) An online seller who supports others members of the Scanner Monkey community (and beyond) while having fun and making money!

Short tail products
1) Products that sell quicker online due to their popularity. See also *Fast Nickel*.
2) Opposite of long tail products.

Slow dime - A product that sells slowly, but returns a higher profit margin.

Traveltage
1) Travel + Arbitrage = Traveltage
2) Sourcing, listing, packing, or shipping while away from home.

Tribe – A group or community of Scanner Monkeys.

Win-win – "Win-win sees life as a cooperative arena, not a competitive one. Win-win is a frame of mind and heart that constantly seeks mutual benefit in all human interactions. Win-win means agreements or solutions are mutually beneficial and satisfying." - Stephen Covey

Commonly Used Acronyms

ATOP = At Time Of Posting. Generally refers to the price on a product at that particular point in time.

AZ = Amazon

FBA = Fulfillment By Amazon

HTF = Hard to Find

LTH = Long Term Hold

MF = Merchant Fulfilled

ROI = Return on Investment

VA = Virtual Assistant

YMMV = Your Mileage May Vary

Chapter 14 – Top 20 Scanner Monkey Phrases

If you're like me, then you probably find yourself saying the same things about what we do as resellers almost every day. There are just certain things that a Scanner Monkey says that few other people in other lines of work would **ever** say. [*Reprinted from our Facebook post in Dec 2013*].

For your entertainment I have compiled a list of the top 20 things a Scanner Monkey says:

#20 – "Honey, I'm only gonna run into this store for 5 minutes and scan a few toys." (an utter lie) – Jay Bayne

#19 – "I'm not really a hoarder; as soon as I get this stuff sent in my basement will be clean." – Julie Cruze

#18 – "No those aren't for me!" (to a cashier after cleaning out a particular brand of foundation powder from the makeup counter of a local pharmacy). – Gilberto Gil

#17 - "I have to get these toys prepped and boxed before my kids see them and I start losing inventory." – Curtis Batdorf

#16 - "OMG, Honey! Come here! You have to see this price" (referring to the price on the scanning app on the phone). – Steve Brown

#15 - "Hey wifey pooh..wanna play Scan This tonight?" – Al Craig

#14 – "No. Sorry. I don't work here." (to several customers that see you scanning in the store) – Duane Malek

#13 - "Yes, actually I *will* need some help getting these 9 carts to my van." – Rachel Lewis-Rapier

#12 - "I wonder how many boxes will fit in my car if I remove the seats?" – Gilberto Gil

#10 – "Where's the ladder?" (to get to all the "treasure" stored at the top of the shelves) – Duane Malek

#9 – "Just let me pack one more box, and then I'll come to bed." – Jay Bayne

#8 – "That coffee is not for you...that is inventory!" – Patty Graves

#7 - "Is that UPS?" (to the sound of any diesel truck within 3 blocks of the house) – Brad DeGraw

#6 – "You stay here...I am going to need another cart, or two, or three." – Julie Cruze

#5 – "Do you have any more in the back?" – Nidia Ramos Espinosa

#4 – "I'm heading to the store to pick up 2 dozens dolls, anyone want anything while I am out?" – Brian Vienneau

#3 – "Just get Chris Green's book!" (after trying unsuccessfully to explain what we do to people that are interested in becoming online sellers) – Jay Bayne

#2 – "Hey look...I've moved the couch and found more inventory!" – Jay Bayne

#1 – "Yes, I'm buying 20 packs of condoms and 10 boxes of pregnancy tests...Makes sense to me!" – Stephen Smotherman

The Scanner Monkey Way

Chapter 15 – Fun with BOLOs

Within the BOLO vernacular there are some lesser known (and sometimes humorous) types of BOLOs we share with each other as Scanner Monkeys. Here is just a sample of some of those more unique BOLOs:

DOH!-LO = "DOH! (Homer Simpson voice) BOLO": A disappointing BOLO, a product that, at first glance, seems to be a real profitable item to resell, but upon further inspection turns out to be a dud. (examples: past expiration date, has damaged packaging, etc..)

eBOLO = eBay BOLO: An item that may not necessarily fetch a profit on Amazon, but can flipped on eBay for good money.

FAUX-LO = faux BOLO: A product that appears to be profitable to resell when compared to a highest priced offering of the same product on Amazon or eBay. However, that high priced item is a listing created by a seller to artificially inflate the price and most likely will not sell at such a ridiculously high price.

IMPOSSIBOLO = Impossible BOLO: [Cue the "Mission Impossible" music]. Your mission, if you choose to accept it, will be to try and locate this extremely hard to find product. Although it is very unlikely that another buyer will locate this item, it is good to share so that others can search for similar type items that may be profitable as well.

MOLO = Maybe a BOLO?: Products that MIGHT be profitable to resell, depending on the circumstances (ie price is right, rank is good, etc..)

The Scanner Monkey Way

NOLO = NOT a BOLO: Products to avoid because they have a track record of not selling well. These are really more of a "buyer beware" type of BOLO since you will most likely lose money if you try and sell them.

ROLO = Regional BOLO: Products that are only found in select regions of the country.

And last, but certainly not least, if you have BOLO MOJO, then you are gifted with the magical power to find BOLOs **everywhere** you look!

Chapter 16 - Testimonials from Members

You've heard us sing the praises of Scanner Monkey throughout this book. It's not always easy to toot your own horn without sounding too self-serving. We think it's important that you should also hear from some of our members as well, so we've compiled some of our favorite testimonials from the group. This will give you some idea as to what the members enjoy about being part of our tribe:

"BOLOs and ScannerMonkey open up your mind to opportunity and allow you to think 'outside the box' or your limited scouting past, and show you that product is everywhere, and deals are abundant, and allow you to realize that YOU can succeed, no matter where you are, and grow your business!! Go for it!!! Monkeys GO FORWARD..." – Bob Willey

"The thing or things I like most is the willingness to share so unselfishly with everyone [...] and the willingness to help anyone that is having a problem. Someone is always ready to jump in to lend a hand." – Donald Shaefer

"I love reading about my fellow monkey's winning buys, especially the newer sellers. It's almost like being a kid on Christmas morning as I can imagine their faces lighting up when they make that first score and they start to truly believe I CAN DO THIS!!!!!!" – Theresa Carlton

"[I like the] willingness of everyone to share excellent info, the humor of so many posts and overall positive and uplifting vibes that are hard to find elsewhere. [I] also feel it is an excellent venue for a newbie like myself to learn the tricks of the trade so I can contribute more in the future and grow my business to be self sufficient." – Christopher du Lys

"Abundance vs Scarcity mindsets! I see so many other groups where everyone is worried about supply of products and tanking prices from those 'damn noobs who give away their sources.' This group embraces abundance and knows that there are plenty of bananas for everyone!" – Rob Walling

"I like it because I can say and do whatever I please without being scolded and laughed at. I love that I can share my adventures and scores with some of the best people that sell on Amazon with FBA and like monkeys. I think Jay was bang on, when he said there was a need for a lounge - this is it and I am not the only one drinking the Kool Aid." – Brian Vienneau

"I love this tribe of monkeys because we know we are all in this crazy Amazon thing together! We can either do it on our own or help each other climb to the top of the banana tree!" – Gail Rosenke

"I love it because it has reignited the fire in my belly. I am having fun. Thank you, fellow Scanner Monkeys. I like seeing posts from fellow Scanner Monkeys on this forum as much as seeing 'Amazon has shipped your item' notifications." – John Groleau

"Sometimes it not THE BOLO that makes me $$, but the direction in which it sends my mind. Are there accessories? Other parts to the line? Similar items that also sell well?" – Avery Naomi Bernstein

"Having the BOLO in hand certainly can make shopping more efficient, but more importantly, it also provides an idea framework that has accelerated my own shopping knowledge. Teach a monkey to fish...." – Lora Lee Hart

"What I love about this group is that we are all part of a true revolution. Jay Bayne, with the help of so many here, has turned the scarcity paradigm into an abundance mindset. I will be honest - I was starting to feel like retail arbitrage was stealing my soul, until this group came along and put the fun back into sourcing. To me, it's like the scene in *The Wizard of Oz*, with the song 'Ding-Dong! The Witch Is Dead.' The munchkins are us, the monkeys, and the 'wicked witch' is the 'all other sellers are my enemy' mindset that has dominated online selling." – Karin Isgur Bergsagel

"I love the personality of this group. Just because it's a business doesn't mean you can't have a good time 'monkeying' around!" – Nancy Cooper Apfel

"I love that this group is so active and so positive. It is the first Facebook group I have been in that I care about every single post here." – Sarah McDougall

"This group is always upbeat, always helpful, good mix of newbies and veterans, so much knowledge freely given, so much love and caring...a goldmine in every aspect!" – Shari Wagner

"This group exudes a true family feeling and a sense of belonging for me. My life is busy, as is everyone else's here, I can stop by when I can, contribute when I can, and pick up on the incredibly wonderful and positive vibes that come from the Scanner Monkey group without feeling scrutinized. It feels like 'coming home'. Love you guys!" – Tonya Nelson

"I love this group because it gives me something to look forward to everyday, like checking the mailbox or going on a treasure hunt! Also, you fellow monkeys are very kind, helpful, inspiring and treat everyone as an equal no matter if you're a newbie or a pro. Thank you!" – Leslie Filinger

"I never really got the whole Facebook group thing until I joined Scanner Monkey. It is like a good book that you cannot put down! I keep going back for more. As a newbie to FBA, I am sure I have made some uneducated comments, but no one makes you feel that way. It is like family! I look forward to the day that I can give as much as I receive. Go Scanner Monkeys!" – Brenda Guidry

"I love the fact that so many sellers offer up so many great items that they have come across in their sourcing. I do not go out hunting BOLOS as my business model but seeing the items from the group puts the mental pictures of them in my mind. When I am out sourcing I have a better chance of spotting the items due to the posts. I have found several items I would have otherwise overlooked plus many more related items to go along with it. A sharing group like this helps to broaden my scouting range greatly. Monkey on!" – James Hoagland

"Some may see a yearly fee to be a Scanner Monkey and not know what to think. I can tell you that from just one BOLO post, I more than paid for my membership fees for the next ten years. Not only can you make money with the BOLO posts, but you can also increase your bottom line by learning from the experiences of others in the group." – Stephen Smotherman

"Thank you for all the invaluable advice and suggestions. I swear every day on this [Scanner Monkey] forum, and the BOLO Exchange that I learn something that improves my business. I've met some great people and formed fantastic relationships. I hope to keep growing with you all!" - Ann Spidalette Sobczak

"I like this group because taking a picture of my monkey in public is not frowned upon. It's actually encouraged." – Mark Freeman

The Scanner Monkey Way

Recommended Resources and Links

Scanner Monkey Links & Resources

- 🍌 Scanner Monkey website:
  http://scannermonkey.com
- 🍌 Scanner Monkey Facebook Group for members:
  https://www.facebook.com/groups/scannermonkey/
- 🍌 Scanner Monkey Facebook Page for anyone:
  https://www.facebook.com/scannermonkey
- 🍌 BOLO Exchange Facebook group:
  https://www.facebook.com/groups/BoloExchange/
- 🍌 Scanner Monkey New Member Tutorial
  https://www.youtube.com/watch?v=gkSCtF63XeE
- 🍌 BOLO Exchange Tutorial:
  http://scannermonkey.com/boloexchange/

PROMO CODE!

Want to join the Scanner Monkey fun? As a token of our appreciation for reading our book, we are going to give you 15% off your 1st year membership or lifetime membership with Scanner Monkey. Just sign up here to receive your coupon code (plus you will receive our free newsletter with tips and updates):

http://scannermonkey.com/bookdiscount

Other Amazing Online Selling Facebook Groups (All Free)

- **Scanpower** - Chris Green's community for Amazon (FBA) and eBay sellers.
  https://www.facebook.com/groups/scanpower/
- **Fast Turn Radio** – Duane Malek's community to discuss strategies for finding and selling fast turn inventory.
  https://www.facebook.com/groups/FastTurnRadio/
- **Thrifting For Profit** – Debra Conrad's group of Amazon FBA sellers that source new and used inventory to resell on Amazon FBA.
  https://www.facebook.com/groups/thriftingforprofit/
- **Thrifting With The Boys** – Run by Jason T. Smith and Bryan Goodman, this is a group page for sharing tips, hints, and ideas about thrift store shopping with the goal of reselling the treasures found.
  https://www.facebook.com/ThriftingWithTheBoys
- **International Selling Insights** - Barrington McIntosh's group with discussions related to International and multi-channel selling.
  https://www.facebook.com/groups/InternationalSelling Insights/
- **My Silent Team** – Jim Cockrum's support group where you can learn to sell on Amazon and eBay or expand your audience and influence online or create great content or books.
  https://www.facebook.com/groups/mysilentteam/

The Scanner Monkey Way

Apps/Software (Discounts available on ScannerMonkey.com)

- 🍌 **ScanPower** - premiere suite of scouting, listing, and repricing software
- 🍌 **InventoryLab** - accounting, listing, and web scouting software
- 🍌 **AppEagle** - repricing service
- 🍌 **Repricit** - repricing service
- 🍌 **Tax Jar** – eCommerce sales tax reporting

Recommended Courses

- 🍌 **ScanPowerU.com** – Led by Chris Green and Duane Malek, this is the one-stop FAST TRACK to getting started with Amazon and FBA (Fulfillment By Amazon)!
- 🍌 **JessicaLarrew.com** – Jessica offers a full array of courses covering topics from sourcing groceries and liquidation inventory to online and retail arbitrage.
- 🍌 **Proven Amazon Course** – considered to be the most comprehensive "selling on Amazon.com" course in the world and the largest expert monitored Amazon selling discussion forum in the world. http://www.mysilentteam.com/public/Introducing_the_Amazing_Fulfillment_by_Amazon_Course.cfm
- 🍌 **Shop Retail, Sell on Amazon** [video at http://bit.ly/1oa70Tb] - Cynthia Stine walks the viewer through an actual shopping trip and explains how to look for inventory in a standard store

Recommended Books (all available on Amazon)

- *Arbitrage: The authoritative guide on how it works, why it works, and how it can work for you*, Chris Green
- *Online Arbitrage: Sourcing Secrets for buying products online to resell for BIG PROFITS*, Chris Green
- *Make Thousands on Amazon in 10 Hours a Week! Revised: How I Turned $200 into $40,000 Gross Sales My First Year in Part-Time Online Sales!*, Cynthia Stine
- *Amazon Autopilot: How to Start an Online Bookselling Business with Fulfillment by Amazon (Fba), and Let Them Do the Work*, Peter Valley
- *The Truth About Retail Arbitrage BOLO's and Their Effect on The Marketplace*, Al Craig and Brian Bly
- *Barcode Booty: How I found and sold $2 million of 'junk' on eBay and Amazon, And you can, too, using your phone*, Steven Weber

Recommended Blogs

- Full Time FBA by Stephen Smotherman http://FullTimeFBA.com
- Online Sales Step by Step by Cynthia Stine http://onlinesalesstepbystep.com/
- Skip McGrath's Online Auction Resource by Skip McGrath http://www.skipmcgrath.com/

Thank you for reading *The Scanner Monkey Way* and please stay in touch at www.ScannerMonkey.com. MONKEY ON!!

About the Authors

Jay Bayne

"Chief Monkey in Charge"

Jay started selling on Amazon FBA under the store name "Shopper Monkey" in October 2012. He spent every spare moment absorbing as much information as possible about running a successful FBA business, which included listening to podcasts, buying books, courses, and coaching. Plus, like many others, he would often ask questions and seek out advice from members of various online seller Facebook groups.

Armed with this knowledge, he was able to sell over $100k in product in his first year. He did all of this while working part time hours around a full time job – utilizing retail arbitrage and some wholesale sourcing.

Jay has over 20 years of experience in sales and marketing in industries as varied as financial services, title insurance, email marketing, and most recently, wine and spirits.

Jay now spends most of his time scanning, sourcing, and listing product for his Amazon store or moderating discussions with the barrel of monkeys in the Facebook group. He lives in the jungle metropolis of Houston, Texas, with his beautiful wife and three little monkeys (two daughters and one son).

He can be reached at: Jay@ScannerMonkey.com

Cordelia Blake

"Right Hand Monkey"

Cordelia, a relatively new, part time Amazon seller, was one of the original "Scanner Monkey Ambassadors." She subscribes to the belief that online sellers could benefit from sharing BOLOs and information in a group setting.

She has a background in sales, marketing, web design, and technology support.

She is a serial entrepreneur and has had some fun jobs including software trainer, costume designer, and science museum educator. She initially approached Jay to help with the BOLOG ("BOLO BLOG") format and has been his right hand monkey ever since.

When she is not earning bananas or playing with the monkeys in the Facebook group, she is herding her own team of gorillas in Atlanta – two sons (ages 3 and 11) and a husband.

She can be reached at: Cordelia@ScannerMonkey.com